I0169285

THE ALL NEW STYLE OF MAGAZINE-BOOKS

SDM LIVE®

www.SDMLIVE.com

MP

MOCY PUBLISHING
WWW.MOCYPUBLISHING.COM

Copyright © 2017 SDM Live.
a division of Mocy Music Publishing, LLC and
C'Cliche, LLC. All rights reserved.
Printed in the U.S.A.

Printed by CreateSpace, An Amazon.com Company

HEALTH & NUTRITIONS, LLC

30 DAYS TO HEALTHY LIVING AND BEYOND.

ARBONNE.®

INDEPENDENT CONSULTANT

WE OFFER HEALTHIER LIFESTYLE WITH ARBONNE PRODUCTS. PLEASE CONTACT BELOW FOR MORE INFORMATION ABOUT ARBONNE PRODUCTS.

PH: (248) 246-6355 | FAX: (248) 436-8360

VISIT US @ HEALTHANDNUTRITIONS.ORG

.site .email .church .web .com .nyc .mobile

TOP Quality

GET A FREE DOMAIN FOR YOUR WEBSITE!!!

FREE WITH EVERY HOSTING PLAN

5DSHOST

THE BEST FOR HOSTING

WWW.5DSHOST.COM

SDM LIVE®

EDITOR-IN-CHIEF
D. "Casino" Bailey
casino@sdmlive.com

EDITORIAL DIRECTOR
Sheree Cranford
sheree@sdmlive.com

GRAPHIC/WEB DESIGNER
D. "Casino" Bailey
casino@sdmlive.com

ACCOUNT EXECUTIVE
Frank Harvest Jr.
frank@sdmlive.com

PHOTOGRAPHERS
Anterlon Terrell Fritz
Treagen Colston
Terance Drake

CONTRIBUTORS
April Smiley
Courtney Benjamin

COPY ORDERS & ADVERTISING OFFICE
Send Money Order or Check to:
Mocy Publishing
P.O. Box 35195
Detroit, Michigan 48235
(833) SDM-LIVE
advertise@sdmlive.com

Copy Order Item
SDM Live Magazine Issue #18
S&H Plus Retail Price - $9.99 per copy

WWW.SDMLIVE.COM

Printed by CreateSpace, An Amazon.com Company

MP
MOCY PUBLISHING

Copyright © 2017 Support Detroit Movement,
a division of Mocy Music Publishing, LLC and
C'Cliche, LLC. All rights reserved.
Printed in the U.S.A.

NO PART OF SDM MAGAZINE, INCLUDING STORIES, ARTWORK, ADVERTISING, OR PHOTO'S MAY BE REPRODUCED BY ANY MEANS WITHOUT THE PRIOR WRITTEN CONSENT FROM MOCY PUBLISHING, LLC. SDM MAGAZINE IS PUBLISHED BY MOCY PUBLISHING, LLC. SDM MAGAZINE WILL NOT ACCEPT ADVERTISING WHICH IS FOUND TO VIOLATE LOCAL, STATE OR FEDERAL LAW.

REAL MUSIC. REAL ENTERTAINMENT.
SDM LIVE®
ISSUE 18

DJ DIZ DRE
TAKING UNDERGROUND MUSIC AND DEJAYING TO A NEW LEVEL

TAMIKA WALKER
CREATING AN EMPIRE WITH HER BOUTIQUE, VACATION BUSINESS AND BRAND NEW RADIO SHOW

ALSO
J SULLI
LEON TAYLOR
DL COLLINS
SINGER REIGN
MR. LIGHT SHOW

L's WITA L & PRODUCER MAC MAN "THE DIRTYMACIN TAKEOVER" 2018

WWW.SDMLIVE.COM

5DSHOST®
THE BEST FOR HOSTING

Get a Website for only $3.99/mo.

GET STARTED

@ WWW.5DSHOST.COM TODAY!

CONTENTS

pg. 12

DJ DIZ DRE
who is that Dj
everyone is talking
about worldwide

pg. 16

L'S WITA L
the Dirtymacin
Takeover for 2018
is in gear

pg. 20

TAMIKA WALKER
new radio show,
travel agent and
boutique launch

pg. 23

TOP 10 CHARTS
The hottest albums
and digital singles
this month features
Akinyele The Blk Night,
Demi Lavato and more.

1

Insignia™ - Qi Certified Wireless Charging Pad for iPhone® - Black
$39.99
www.bestbuy.com

2

Apple - iPhone X 64GB - Space Gray (Sprint)
$47.92/mo
www.bestbuy.com

3

Gemini - 2-Channel Virtual DJ Controller
$279.99
www.bestbuy.com

GET AN SSL CERTIFICATE ON YOUR WORDPRESS WEBSITE AND START ACCEPTING CREDIT AND DEBIT CARDS TODAY!

An SSL Certificate on your website will secure your customers data using encryption technology.

5DSHOST®
THE BEST FOR HOSTING

Also open an account at Stripe.com to start collecting funds from your secure Wordpress website. It's FREE!

www.5DSHOST.com

GET A FREE DOMAIN WITH HOSTING PLAN
as low as $3.99 a month.

10% OFF COUPON CODE: GET10OFF

5DSHOST®
THE BEST FOR HOSTING

www.5DSHOST.com

cPanel®

FiNDDU
Fashion.COM
CATERING TO THE EVERYDAY WOMAN.

DRESSLINGERIEBEZZLE
SWIM WEARCORSETS
PLUS SIZESGOWNS
CALL FOR CUSTOM DESIGN (313) 293-1690

Spirit of the Bronx

THIS IS HOW THE DETROIT CITY COUNCIL DOESN'T EMBODY THE SPIRIT OF DETROIT WITH ITS 2017 RECIPIENTS

by Cheraee C.

Just recently rapper Cardi B received a 2017 Spirit of Detroit Award. Detroiters instantly jumped to social media infuriated and disrespected by their city. There's nothing symbolic about ignoring and misrepresenting the talent in your city. The city council should've denied the request to give Cardi B a spirit award. Her growing success and music industry accomplishments don't have anything to do with the citizens and issues in Detroit, Michigan.

The city council needs to revisit the Spirit of Detroit Award's criteria and tighten up its standards. We have so many billionaires and noteworthy people in our city who deserve recognition. If the city council wants to give away awards to people who aren't natives or citizens of Detroit, or to people who haven't invested millions or billions in our city then city council needs to rename the Spirit of Detroit Award to something more general and basic.

Celebrity Tell-All

ACTRESS GABRIELLE UNION BEARS IT ALL IN HER NEW, EXCLUSIVE TELL-ALL BOOK.

by Cheraee C.

Actress Gabrielle Union can now add best-selling author to her long list of accomplishments. Her debut book is full of all types of unbelievable confessions and experiences. Who knew Gabrielle struggled with fertility, discrimination, abuse, and many other issues the average woman endures?

There was no holding back in this book. Gabrielle even opens about sex and her opinions about it in general, in a relationship, and masturbation. Some people were offended by Gabrielle's openness saying that she should've kept her private life private. Much like we see Gabrielle in the millions of roles she has played on the screen, she always keeps it real. If anything she is showing other women and other celebrities why they shouldn't be afraid or embarrassed of their truth.

We're Going To Need More Wine
By Gabrielle Union

Available from Amazon.com and other online stores

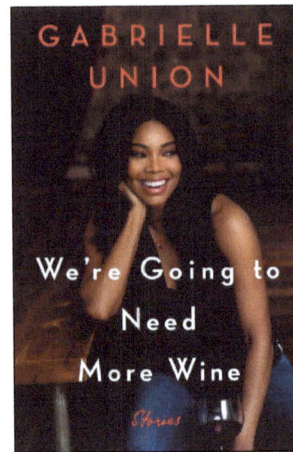

MOCY PUBLISHING PRESENTS

CHERAEE C.
The Queen Pen

GET YOUR BOOK PUBLISHED or EDITED TODAY!

FUNDS2HELP
MAKING A CHANGE TOGETHER

Funds2Help.com is a place where people can get help with crowdfunding, business funding, personal funding and more. Funds are donated instantly to users Paypal account with no waiting time.

www.Funds2Help.com

Yo That's My Dj

MAKING NEW AVENUES FOR NEW ARTISTS IN THE STREETS GLOBALLY
AND LOCALLY WHILE BRANDING WHOISDJDIZDRE.COM
by Cheraee C.

Q. When did you realize you wanted to become a DJ and do you plan to become a part of any DJ movements?

A. I always knew that I wanted to be a DJ when I used to listen to my mom playing music around the house at a young age. I would use her CD collection and take the best old school classic songs and make my own playlist. Then we would have family functions on the weekend and I would play my mix CD that I made from her collection for the family and friends. Also, my uncle was a known DJ in the city and I was influenced by him. So pretty much that's when I knew I wanted to take this to the next level because I enjoyed entertaining people.

Q. How did you get involved with SDM Live Radio and how do you like working on this outlet?

A.I got involved with SDM Live Radio from a friend of mines that's also a DJ. He introduced me to Casino and the rest was history. I really enjoy working for SDM Live Radio because it gives me a lot of opportunities and I can showcase my talent. This company is an awesome format to work for and it has a bright future

Q. You covered a lot of events and festivals this year around Detroit. What event or festival was your favorite to DJ and why?

A.I got a chance to be part of the Detroit 2017 Electronic Movement Festival. It was a great experience because the music was different and I always wanted to be part of the EDM movement. I am a very diverse DJ and I enjoy playing different galleries of music so that was a good experience to be part of.

Q. You also dedicated a lot of mixes to national events such as your 2pac mix dedicated to 2pac upon his birthday and the release of his biopic. What national event do you plan to cover next and why?

A.As a DJ I try to stay connected with the music and different things that goes on in the industry. I thought it would be cool to do that Tupac mix because everybody was anticipating his biopic and it was perfect because it dropped on his birthday. I got a lot of events that I want to cover. I just pretty much go by whatever is trending at the time. I will soon be releasing a collection of mixtapes with different artists that people will enjoy.

Q. As a DJ do you plan to focus more on breaking out new artists, playing Detroit music, mixtapes, or just exposure and why?

A.I try to stay connected with the new talent that comes out nationwide and also the local artists because I know the artists are counting on the DJs to promote their music. A DJ plays a big role in breaking new talent, so I try to stay connected with new music outlets like SpinFire which gives the artist the opportunity to get their music played worldwide in clubs, and also radio. I definitely want to stay connected with the local

artists in my city so I'm able to break their music.

Q. What career move/change or project are you looking forward to do most within the next six months?

A.I'm trying to do something different in the future by dropping a mixtape album and I'm looking to put out a new single for my project soon entitled Press Play. I also have a production team (Dirty Macin Pro) and we have local talent that we're working with. I'm also trying to launch a new clothing line soon so definitely look out for that. Stay tuned for the different things I got coming up in the future. I just want to continue playing good music for the people and showcase my talent worldwide for different genres.

Branding Diamonds

MOVIE PRODUCER DL COLLINS IS MOTIVATING THE STREETS
WITH HER NEW LESBIAN REALITY SHOW BASED OUT OF DETROIT

by Cheraee C.

Q. What made you want to do your own reality show?

A. Every time my wife and I are out we are always bombarded with tons of questions about how we run our household and since I knew years ago that I wanted to get into film I decided that I could kill two birds with one stone and give people a peek into our world and fulfill my goal as a filmmaker.

Q. Can you tell us about your reality show, what is it called? What is it about?

A. It's called More Than Just Us and it's about eight lesbian friends fighting for success in love, family, and career.

Q. When you film Season 2 do you plan to get new couples or are you going to reuse the same couples?

A. Season 2 we will definitely bring in another couple or two, but you will have to wait until the end of Season 1 to see if we have anyone leaving.

Q. Do you think you and your cast will inspire more lesbians to do reality shows and be more open about their sexuality and relationships?

A. I hope so (laughing) my goal is to give us a voice. Allow us the opportunity to show that we are normal in all that we do.

Q. What irritates you most about modern lesbians and modern lesbian relationships?

A. I won't say it irritates me, but I get frustrated with the gender roles. The rules we set forth for who we are and who we have to be. I think that modern lesbians are so worried about pleasing the world that they lose sight of who they really are and that's women who love women.

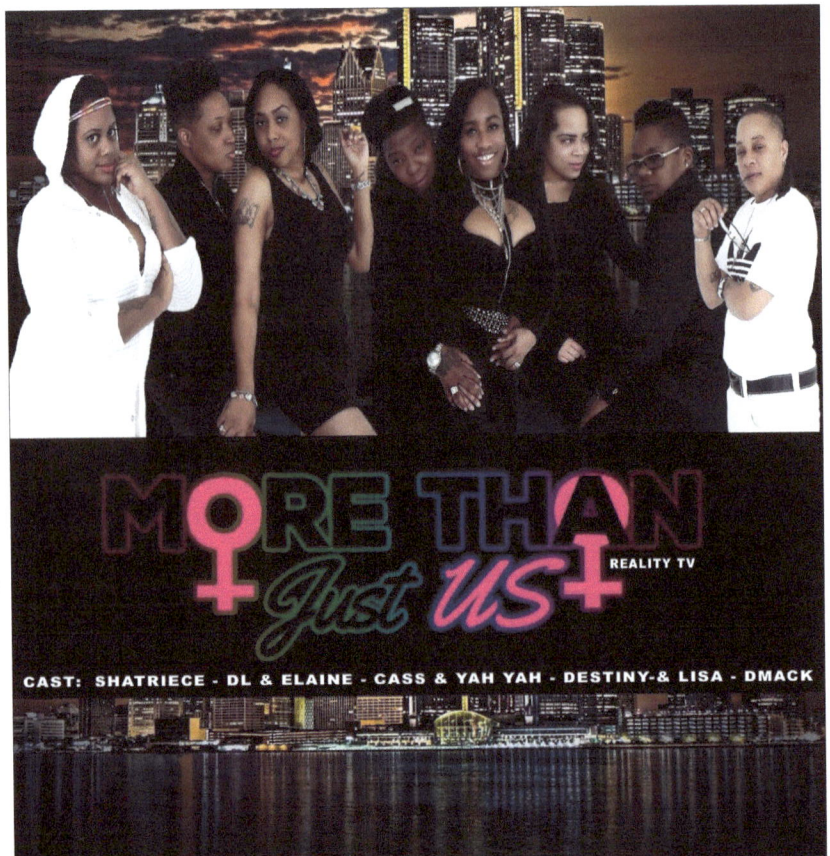

CAST: SHATRIECE - DL & ELAINE - CASS & YAH YAH - DESTINY-& LISA - DMACK

Upscale, VIP Status

MR. LIGHT SHOW IS THE FIRST MOBILE DJ IN MICHIGAN TO EXEMPLIFY THE BEAUTY OF PRESENTATION AND AMBIANCE AT CORPORATE EVENTS.

by: Cheraee C.

Q. For those who don't know, what is your business? What do you do as an entrepreneur?

A. I own a mobile DJ company, C. Smith Entertainment, LLC. I provide upscale DJ services for weddings, private parties, and corporate events.

Q. What made you get into providing upscale DJ services?

A. I started out like any other DJ with just the basics; turntables, speakers, and a laptop. I felt like something was missing though. So, I started looking at DJ's in Texas and Florida and how they focused on presentation. So, I researched different things I could use to create a better presentation and ambiance. I was the first mobile DJ in Michigan to provide the presentation and the ambiance at weddings. Presentation, as in a DJ booth that hid all of my wires and matched the clients wedding colors. Ambiance, as in uplighting and other mood lighting to match their colors as well.

Q. How'd you get the nickname Mr. Light Show?

A. I bought a set of lights that just came out that were really expensive and looked like some futuristic stuff, and my homeboy said, "okay I see you Mr. Light Show," so I ran with it.

Q. What is one of the most memorable upscale events that you were a part of in 2017? What was the experience like?

A. I dejayed on the 50 yard line at Ford Field which had the biggest stage of my career. The experience was surreal. Typically, if there's outside DJ's, they have been tucked away up in their booth so to have my booth with my name on it in the middle of the field was special.

Q. If you could DJ at any upcoming celebrity event/wedding who would it be and why?

A. I really wish Gucci Mane would've called me for his! Lol! I'm looking to expand to Atlanta so that would've been a great look. Other than that, if Common and Angela Rye get married, I would love to do that. They're two conscious people that I would love to have a conversation with and be part of their special day.

100% WITH NO CHASER

THE STREETS IS TALINK AND THEY TALKING ABOUT L'S WIT A L AND HOW HE CAN BE THE NEXT UP TO BLOW FROM DETROIT
by Cheraee C.

Q. Out of all the artists you've worked with, who did you vibe with the most and why?

A. I'll have to say Forty Da Great because it's more of a history wanting to do music with him since I was younger.

Q. Did you experience any obstacles in getting collabs with other artists or did you know the artists socially/personally already?

A. Everybody I collab with I know personally more than likely and are fans of their music and they feel the same about me I assume lol so there's never been any obstacles just love and respect.

Q. What would you do if you couldn't do music anymore?

A. That's not an option. I can't even answer that lol I feel it's only right I create music.

Q. Describe your ideal dream setting for creating music (a dream studio, music cave, etc) what would you do in it?

A. Some of the finest studio equipment, a great engineer, my producer, and just a peaceful environment that I have unlimited time to create and record I'll be fine. I don't need a lot to be great just a good sound system and equipment is about it.

Q. What if you got a record deal tomorrow. What is the first thing you'll do with your first check?

A. I would buy some property and invest in my music and products x3 more than I do now and travel more than I do now and travel a few places I never visited to set up more shows and of course have a little fun with the extras.

Q. If you had to change anything about music, what would it be and why?

A. I'll change the type of music radio stations play. I wish radio stations would play more local quality music without changing artists.

Q. How did you get involved with Dirty Macin Pro and how do you feel about that brand?

A. Me and my cousin/producer Mac Man started the label as kids so I feel very passionate about it and I stand behind it 1000%. It's more than just a label it's a movement, it's a lifestyle!

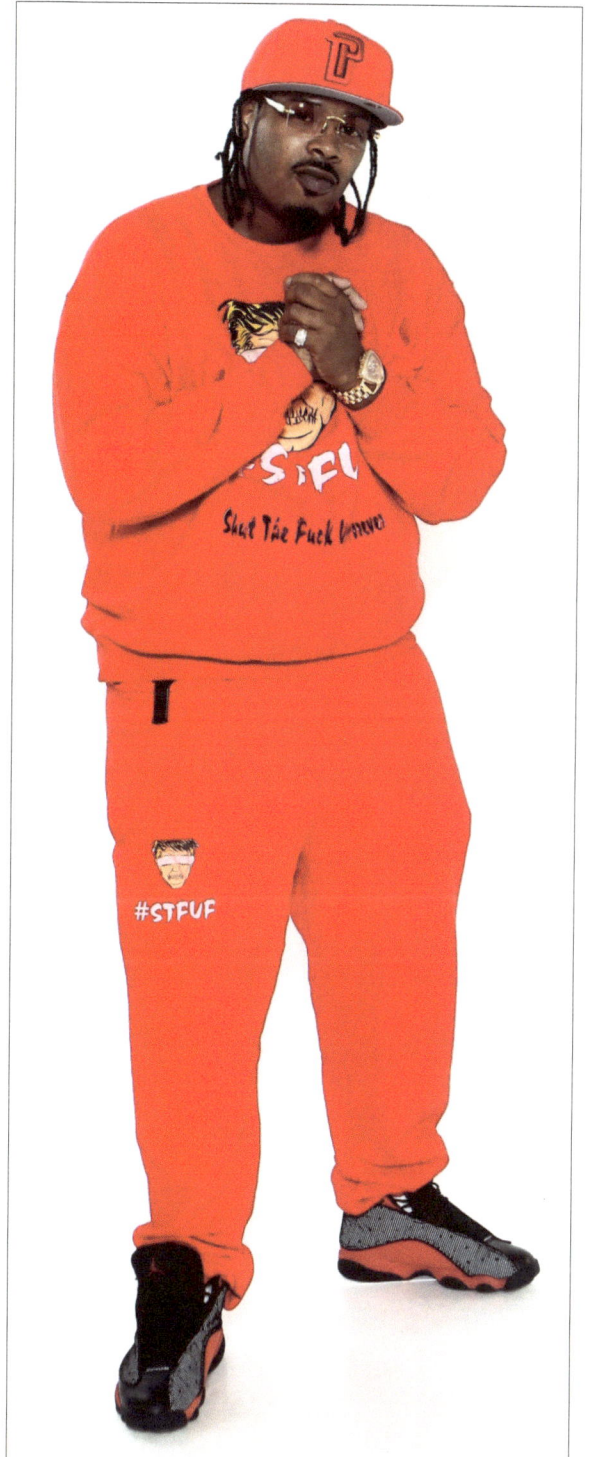

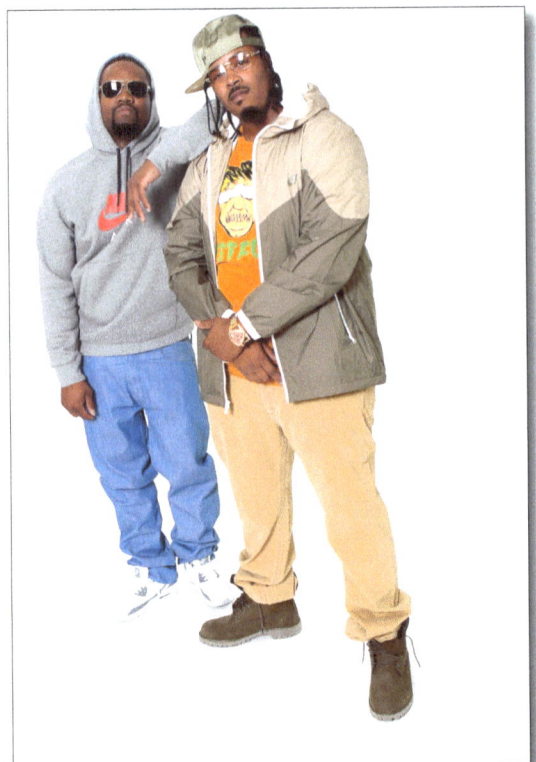

Q. What's your current single and project that you're working on?

A. Besides my latest video STFUF, I'm working on two more videos I'll be releasing by next month called LAST FOREVER and I WANNA SMOKE then I'll be releasing a EP called NO TITLE. I have a full project called Social Media Vol.3 with 14 songs I sale currently, but once I build my buzz and brand more I'll release my next project.

Now watch SDM on Roku TV.
Get access to the SDM Channel
with all new TV Shows, Movies,
VIP Exclusive Events and more.

SDM LIVE®

REAL MUSIC. REAL ENTERTAINMENT.

Search for **SDM** on **Roku TV**

Trouble in the Streets

JAY-Z PENS ON BLACK INJUSTICE

by Semaja Turner

The music world has been going crazy to Meek Mill's recent prison sentencing. Some feel as though he deserved to be imprisoned while others like Jay-Z see his imprisonment as another example of black injustice in the black community. Rapper Jay-Z was so inspired by Meek's story, he wrote an opinionated editorial about the presence and reality of black injustice in the criminal system. Jay-Z makes valid points about how the criminal system is designed to cripple black men. Just because, Meek is a celebrity doesn't mean his crimes should go unpunished. In most cases, money has never been able to buy freedom. Instead it's about looking at the bigger picture and saving our black men from never-ending cycles. Probation violations should be petty crimes and mediocre when we have mass murderers, terrorists, and etc to worry about trying to wipeout races and nations.

Stan'D Funk'y

MOGUL TAMIKA WALKER IS CREATING AN EMPIRE WITH HER BOUTIQUE, VACATION BUSINESS, AND BRAND NEW RADIO SHOW

by Cheraee C.

Q. How'd you find out about SDM Live and how do you feel about their network?

A. One of my good friends works for the station and when she was asked did anyone want their own station I jumped on that opportunity. I felt this was another way of me getting my brand out to the world.

Q. What is the name of your boutique, where is your boutique located, and who is your boutique named after? If you had to rename your boutique again for business purposes would you?

A. Stan'D Funk'y Boutique is located online only at www.tandtboutique.squarespace.com. My boutique is named after my brother Stanley Dewayne. The reason I named it after him is because he passed about four years ago and I wanted his name to live on. I would not rename it. I love the name and the name means so much to me.

Q. Owning a boutique is a popular business trend. Name three things about your boutique that differs from other boutiques.

A. We have great customer service. We do not lie to customers to get a sale. I would rather lose the sale then for our customer to think we only care about the dollar. If they feel confident and sexy in our pieces they will tell at least 3 people but if we lie or don't put them first they will tell 10 and that can damage your brand.

Q. Just recently you launched a t-shirt line. What is the name of the line, what is the price range of your t-shirts, and describe your t-shirts?

A. Our top seller T-Shirt is the "I'm thick and loving it." The reason for this t-shirt was because I wanted all women to feel sexy and comfortable in their skin no matter what size they are and women of all sizes purchase this T-Shirt. All the T-Shirts are $20 and they range from Small to 3X.

Q. What made you want to broadcast your own radio show on SDM Live Radio and what are your feelings about doing your first show?

ENJOY A WESTGATE VACATION!

4 Days & 3 Nights

From **$99**

Plus tax. Restrictions apply.

Book Online: wstgt.com/ **29301009618**

Call: **800-297-2414**

Mention Discount Code: **29301009618**

Choose From:
- Orlando
- Branson
- Gatlinburg
- Park City
- Myrtle Beach
- Las Vegas

WR
WESTGATE RESORTS

This advertising material is being used for the purpose of soliciting sales of timeshare interests.

A. I am nervous, but that comes with anything you do for the first time. The reason that I have chosen to broadcast is because I feel this will help expand my brand and I can help others expand theirs.

Q. When will your show air on SDM Live Radio and what will your radio show focus on?

A. I air every Saturday from 6-7 pm. No topic is off limits. For the month of November my shows will consist of local artists, a friend speaking on feeding the homeless, and last but not least a no limit conservation with a few women.

Q. Do you have any other businesses besides a boutique?

A. I have a vacation business and it is called Presidential Travels and it's a Westgate Travel Partner. They have packages starting at $99 for 4 days and 3 nights and for additional information please call 313-622-1580.

Mr. First Class Fly

WHILE SOME ARTIST PROMOTE NEGATIVE MUSIC, HIP-HOP ARTIST J.SULLI IS ALL ABOUT PROMOTING POSITIVITY AND BEING EPIC.

by No'el Snyder

Q. The music industry is a task. What or who keeps you motivated to do music?

A. Music serves as therapy for me. Success-wise of course like any other usual young man my mother and my family is my "why" for grand success, but music itself is a therapy. I see, hear, and feel music differently from a lot of people.

Q. What made you go vegan? Do you think being vegan is good for your music?

A. Well right now I've only been going vegan for seven days. Still unclear as to how it affects my music, lol. But I can say I went vegan due to research on how it affects the body. Not only that just putting things in perspective. Also, I went vegan so eventually I can help some of my family get healthier, and I believe in setting examples as best as possible.

Q. What is your current goal for your music?

A. Vast exposure. The money will come, but I'm also deeply focused on my branding. Trying to go a little deeper than just the music. Music is a young man's game. I'm not old, but I'm 31 and time is ticking so I want my legacy to extend pass music as well.

Q. Do you think money is the root to fame or just time, connections, etc?

A. Some people get notoriety from a lifestyle of balling, getting money etc. Some people are connected. It depends on the audience you're appealing to. It's all based on how people relate. Either that person relates to what you've been through or some people idolize what you've accomplished and want to attain that. Hell some people just find certain social media virality to be entertaining.

Q. Are you working on any projects now?

A. I am working on a new project. Still in pre-production as of right now, but I do have a freestyle series that I drop every Saturday @12pm EST. It's called Sulli Sparring Sessions" and everyone can catch that on my instagrm @Heirsulli or on y public Facebook page Facebook.com/jdotsulli.

Q. What made you create your freestyle series and what type of feedback have you been getting from it?

A. I created it to re-generate a stronger buzz. I had gone MIA from music for a little bit. With relocating as well as personal situations, music was just low on the list. But now I'm getting back to it. And what better way than to put out "something" on some good quality than to just give announcements.

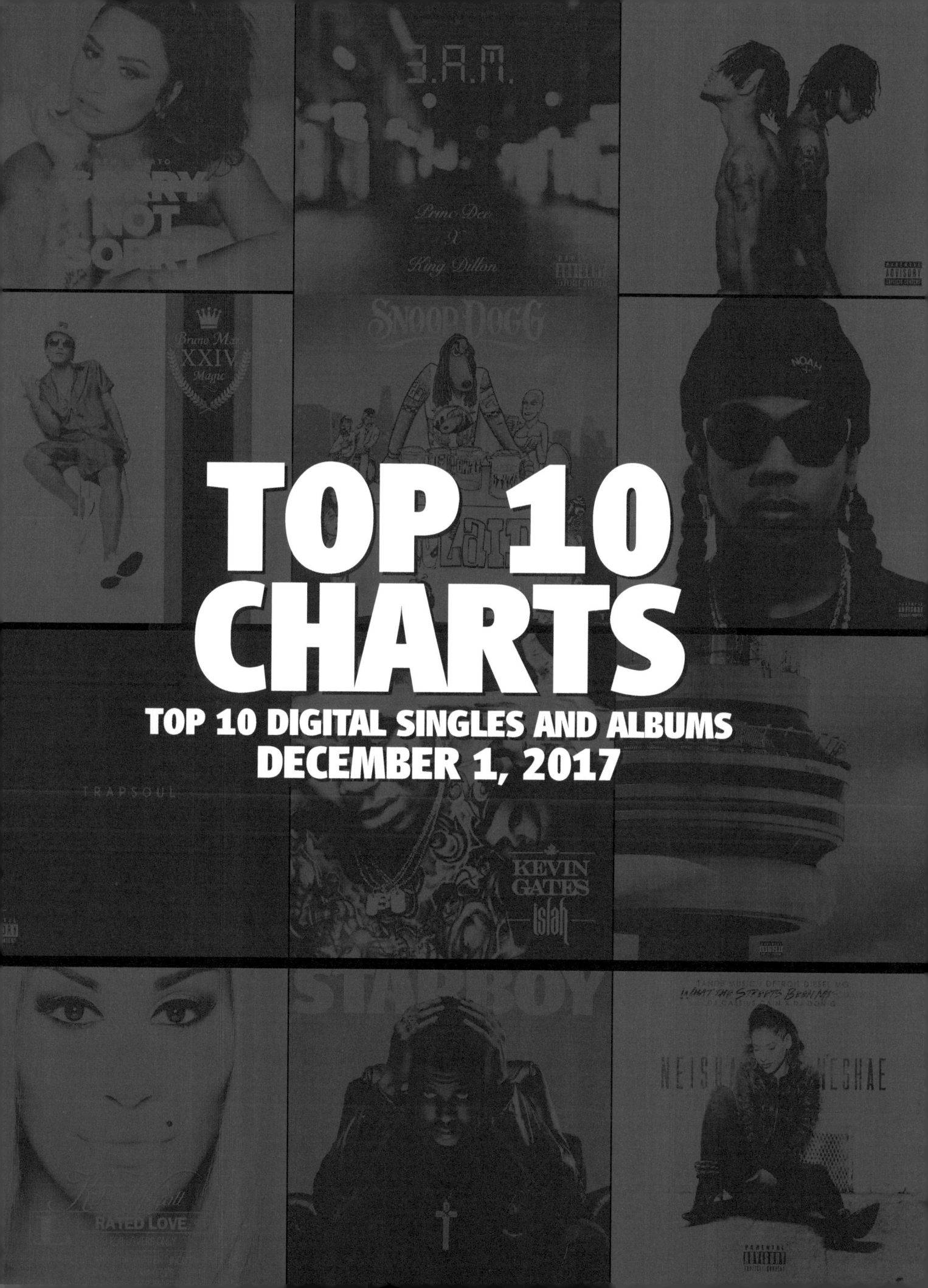

TOP 10 CHARTS

TOP 10 DIGITAL SINGLES AND ALBUMS
DECEMBER 1, 2017

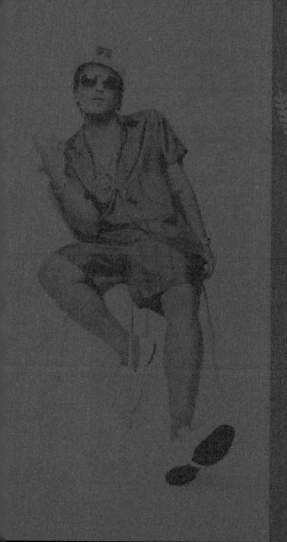

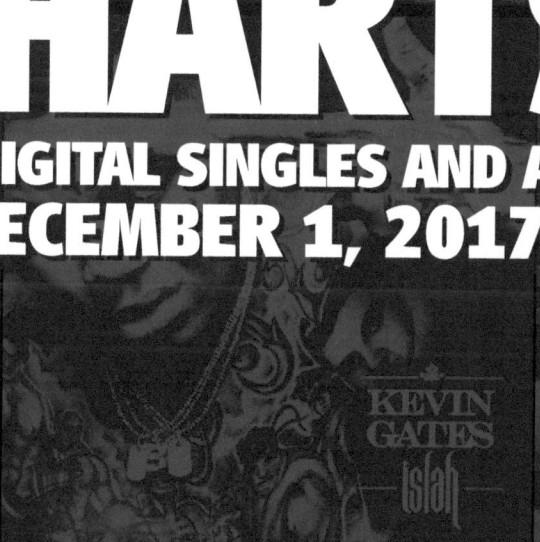

TOP 10 CHARTS

DEMI LOVATO IS 'SORRY NOT SORRY' ABOUT HER RAGING HOUSE PARTY IN NEW VIDEO: WATCH.

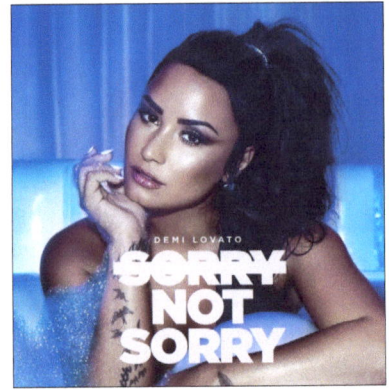

DEMI LOVATO
Sorry Not Sorry
Coming in at #1 this month,
The hottest song on the radio
"Sorry Not Sorry" by Demi Lovato.

TOP 10 SINGLES
CHART OF THE MONTH

No.	Artist - Song Title
1	DEMI LOVATO - SORRY NOT SORRY
2	DJ KAHLED - WILD THOUGHTS
3	FRENCH MONTANA - UNFORGETTABLE
4	KING DILLON - RIVALS
5	YO GOTTI - RAKE IT UP FEATURING NICKI MINAJ
6	JP ONE - MILLION
7	GUCCI MANE - I GET THE BAG FT. MIGOS
8	KHALID - LOCATION
9	21 SAVAGE - BANK ACCOUNT
10	LIL PUMP - GUCCI GANG

TOP 10 ALBUMS
CHART OF THE MONTH

No.	Artist - Album Title
1	AKINYELE THE BLACK NIGHT FAMILY - THE LAST MIXTAPE
2	CHÉ - CHÉNGES
3	KHALID - AMERICAN TEEN
4	LIL UZI VERT - LUV IS RAGE 2
5	21 SAVAGE - ISSA ALBUM
6	KENDRICK LAMAR - DAMN.
7	DRAKE - MORE LIFE
8	DJ KHALED - GIFTFUL
9	MIGOS - CULTURE
10	2 CHAINZ - PRETTY GIRLS LIKE TRAP MUSIC

DO YOU NEED ROADSIDE ASSISTANCE?
only $9.99/mo.
WWW.GETROADSIDENOW.COM

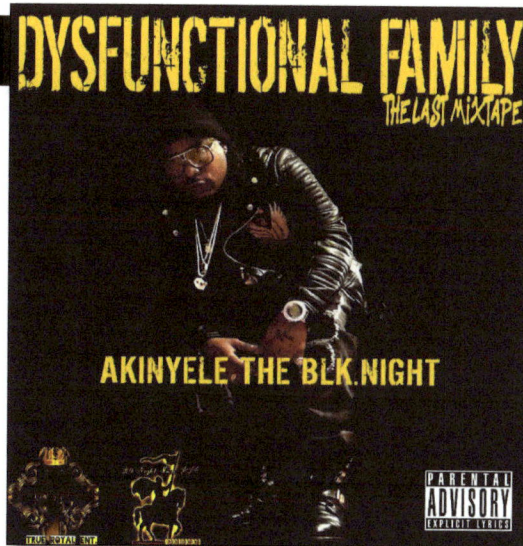

Dysfunctional Family: The Last Mixtape

ARTIST: Akinyele The Blk Night
RATING: 5

The music scene in the city of Detroit not only glorifies the talented artist it inhabits, but also displays the powerful collaborations that can be embodied by building relationships and collective experiences, making for an interesting project. Akinyele The BLK Night, gathers everyone together for his final mixtape, "Dysfunctional Family". Layed over original beats, Mr. Rhythm and Blues adds piano keys with bass for his own originality towards the production. Having firsthand relationships with all eighteen features, Akinyele discusses the passion behind creating great music and the music industries mis- placed sight that captured the original essence of hip-hop and R&B Soul. Tracks such as "Still Winning" featuring Killa Smurf & Big Bus, and "Last Whoorahh" featuring JP One, showcased smoothed out vocals, adding the roughness element and grit derived from the hip hop genre. While other songs such as "R&B Mixtape King" featuring Chris Lanard, and "Lonely" featuring Katrina Carson, demonstrates an emotionally, enriching sound with lyrics that touches the heart of every true R&B listener. Leading into a multitude of other supple R and B songs, "Dysfunctional Family" is a classic R&B mixtape, that captures every element of its genre, all while being touching, relatable, and elegantly firm. Check out Akinyele The BLK Night final mixtape, Dysfunctional Family on Dattpiff!.

"Money and Politics Got It So Tainted. Oh, and They Wanna Dictate All The Music. Half of This Shit That You Hear You Dont Like It. Its Just Overly Played, So Repetitive. Its Only So Long 'Fore You Singing It."

Chénges

ARTIST: Detroit Ché
RATING: 4

While most consider life changes difficult to adjust to, the listener is put at ease and into a tranquil state of mind, as one song effortlessly flows to the next. Ché, formerly known as Detroit Ché, released her highly anticipated EP "Chénges". The 22 year old songstress vocally allows us listeners an intimate glimpse into her thoughts. Ché discusses how being inebriated can conflict with the writing process, addressing oppression within the system and to the young African American men and women that are being controlled by the media who simply need to love themselves as a whole, all while finding happiness within herself. Already musically seasoned Ché, lyrically connects with her melodious production using acoustic guitar, and piano keys, adjacent to low tempo drum kicks done by Adam Depollo, DopeDiv Ali, and Jaye Prime. Ché pays homage to a classic 1996 track, "If I Ruled The World" by Nas featuring Lauryn Hill on her first song "Seed". In doing so, this intro was organically projected, with a sonorous sound that gave appreciation to this classic. The loosely self titled EP "Chénges", came with four metaphorical tracks that symbolize germination and exemplify firm representations of Che's growth as a person and as an artist. It's been a year and five months since her debut EP release "SMALL-

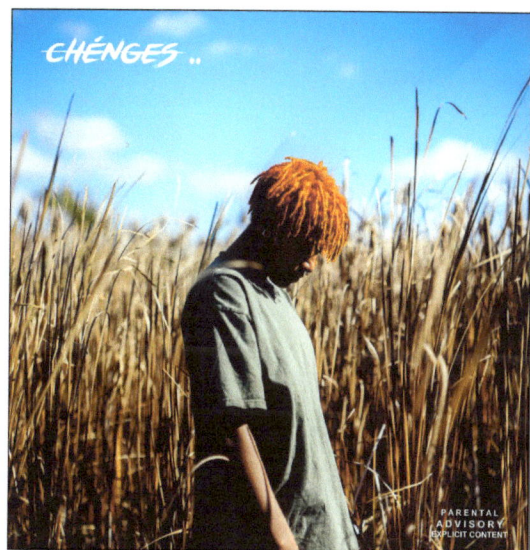

talk", and I speak for all when I say, "Chénges" is packed with uplifting conscious lyrics & soulful vocals, which are enough for repeated listens. If you haven't already, check out Detroit Ché EP "Chénges" on Tidal, Apple Music and Spotify!

"Let's Use Our Energy, Brothers And Sisters, Not Enemies. Let's Love Each Other So Tenderly, Them Proper Way To Make Memories. Now Picture That, Aye, That's Beautiful Imagery, Aye Putcha Hands Up If You Feeling Me...!"

HEELS &
SKILLZ

Shay

is a beautiful model from Detroit, MI that loves playing drums and tennis.

instagram
@shayshayluvingoldenlife95

Photography by
@terancedrake

Simone Stewart

is from Detroit
and enjoys modeling.

instagram
N/A

HEELS &
SKILLZ

Photography by
@terancedrake

HEELS &
SKILLZ

Unbeleivablee

A model in the
movie True Religion
from Detroit MI.

instagram
@_unbeleivablee_

Photography by
@barearmy

REAL MUSIC. REAL ENTERTAINMENT.

SDM

ISSUE 18

DJ DIZ DRE
TAKING UNDERGROUND MUSIC AND DEJAYING TO A NEW LEVEL

TAMIKA WALKER
CREATING AN EMPIRE WITH HER BOUTIQUE, VACATION BUSINESS AND BRAND NEW RADIO SHOW

ALSO
J SULLI
LEON TAYLOR
DL COLLINS
SINGER REIGN
MR. LIGHT SHOW

WWW.SDMLIVE.COM

L's WITA L
& PRODUCER
MAC MAN
"THE DIRTYMACIN TAKEOVER" 2018

5DSHOST®
THE BEST FOR HOSTING

Providing The Best Hosting Experience for Your Company.

10% OFF
CODE: GET10OFF
Limited Time Offer

Bronze Website Hosting Plan
for only $3.99/mo.

GET A FREE DOMAIN
WITH EVERY YEARLY HOSTING PLAN.

www.5DSHost.com

Cheraee's Corner
IN THESE DAYS IN TIME IS THE MUSIC BUSINESS REALLY WORTH IT?
by Cheraee C.

Constantly, we hear artists speaking on the naked truth about the industry. Artists wind up regretting record deals, regretting the fame, and disliking the music business. Then artists speak on the brainwashing of the media and the white-washing of different genres of music in general. Real music has been replaced by society's industry sound.

Any dream is worth the ambition, sweat, and tears, but why focus on being an industry underdog? Why be signed to a record label when you can start your own label? Most celebrities started with nothing and have encountered mass success on their own. Why do we feel like we need money, labels, etc to achieve greatness? All we really need is time, education, and patience.

NEXT 2 BLOW

LEON TAYLOR

Q.

Q. What is your favorite song on your EP "Love Can" and why?

A. My favorite song from my EP is "Amazing" because it just describes what music does to me. Most would think the song is about relations with a woman but it's actually music. Music makes love to my mind through my ears reaching my very soul and it's amazing.

Q. You also just did a joint project with Akinyele the Blk Knight. Do you think more artists should do joint projects and why?

A. It really depends on who you gel with musically and can learn different things from by working together and plus it puts both artists in a place to gain new fans by the merge of the two artists and also making quality music and history and building an artist to artist bond just make sure everyone one is on the same page and everything flows smoothly.

Q. Every time you step out your swag is on 1000. What inspires the way you dress with the hats, blazers, leather, etc?

A. Well my grandfather wears those classy hats and the rest I just looked up and researched R&B artists and how they dress and I just mixed it with what I like to wear with the help of Black Rain of Team Money Hungry he is a great image consultant.

Q. Is it any point in your music career when you wanted to just give it up or quit?

A. No I never wanna quit I believe in there being different times I'm an artist's career when we all have to kind of hibernate and reinvent ourselves to marry ourselves to creativity and developing new styles staying relevant and also different from other artists.

Q. What made you seek management? Do you feel like you get more accomplished with a manager?

A.I knew I wanted a team and someone to take care of the business and booking while allowing me to put 100% into my craft and music giving me time to be as creative as I could giving you all the best of me in every song. Yes I feel like we get more accomplished because we are working on different things that all contribute to the goal of being a great Artist.

Q. What is the craziest experience you ever had singing a song to a girl and why?

A. Once I was sing to a woman serenading her and grinding I sang in her ear next thing you know she took off her thong and put it in my hand. It was the first time that ever happened I was in complete shock very unexpected and that's about it.

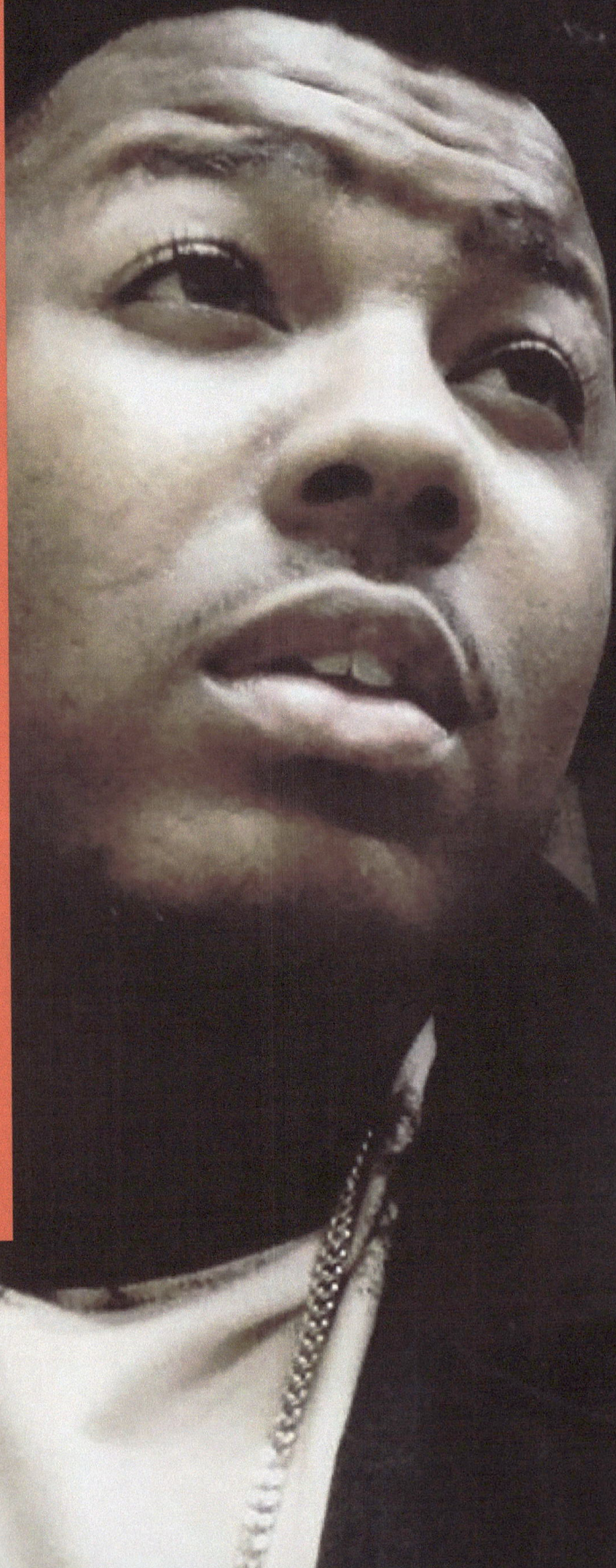

Q.

Q. So Reign I know most people don't like comparisons, but who does most people compare your voice too and why?

A. Jasmine Sullivan and Brandy and I don't really know why to be honest. I think because my voice sounds similar to them and my vibe is also similar.

Q. If you couldn't do music anymore what would you do?

A. I would do modeling and acting.

Q. How do you feel about singers in the Detroit music industry today? Who do you enjoy? Do you feel like it's a competition?

A. I feel likeit's a lot of amazing talent in Detroit that is not noticed. I enjoy Detroit artists such as Marcus Devine, Akinyele The Blk Night, Leon Taylor, Ava Jay Stuart, Glenda Washington, Pierre Anthony, 3xotic, and etc. I could go on and on, but I don't compete I just do me.

Q. When and why did you decide you wanted to take your singing professionally?

A. I decided I wanted to take my music professionally when I was 21. The reason why is because music is what makes my heart beat and this is my dream. I want to make it for my family and I love to make people smile.

Q. Are you going to go on any televised music shows or jst keep trying to hit mainstream by any means?

A. I'm just grinding right now. I don't know what's in store, but Im going to stay focused and keep grinding.

Q. What's one interesting fact about Reign your fans would like to know?

A. I have a big heart, I'm humble, I love to have fun and party, but I'm ambitious.

NEXT 2 BLOW
SINGER REIGN

SNAP SHOTS

Email Your Snap Shots to
snapshots@sdmlive.com

PH: (586) 558-8978
FAX: (586) 558-8979

SPECIAL PRIORITY, LLC.

WWW.SPECIALPRIORITYLLC.COM

LET SPECIAL PRIORITY BE YOUR #1 SOURCE FOR ADULT CARE. WE TAKE PRIDE IN HELPING OUR COMMUNITY.

27170 DEQUINDRE RD WARREN, MI. 48092

WE ALSO SPECIALIZE IN:

- Mental Health Counseling Services
- Substance Abuse Program
- Drug Abuse Program
- Physical Therapy

Urban Fiction, Spiritual, Motivation and more.
Order a book from Mocy Publishing today and receive FREE shipping.

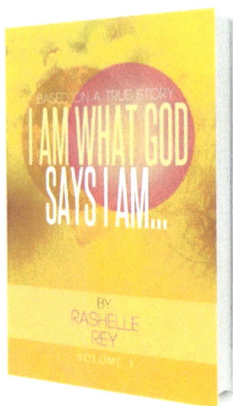

I Am What God Says I Am...
By Rashelle Rey

Item #: IAWGS29
Price: $9.99

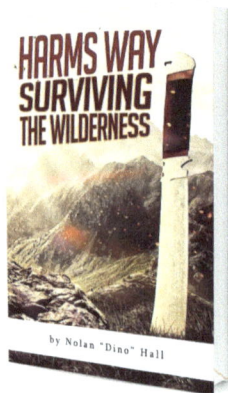

Harm's Way
By Nolan "Dino" Hall

Item #: HWS821
Price: $15.99

The Shadiest Mission Ever
By Cheraee C.

Item #: TSME28
Price: $12.99

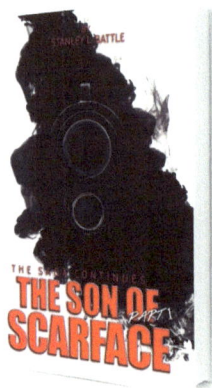

The Son Of Scarface – Part 1
By Stanley L. Battle

Item #: TSOS01
Price: $12.99

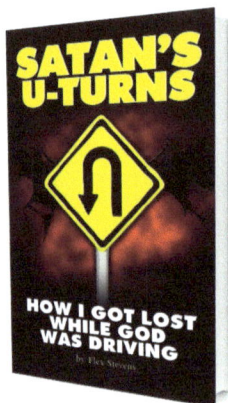

Satan's U-Turns
By Flex Stevens

Item #: SUT382
Price: $9.99

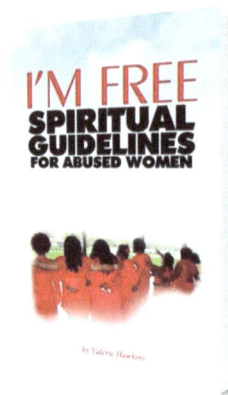

I'm Free
By Valerie Hawkins

Item #: IFTSG82
Price: $14.99

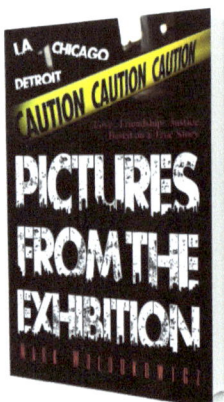

Pictures From The Exhibition
By Mark Wolodkowicz

Item #: PFAE292
Price: $15.99

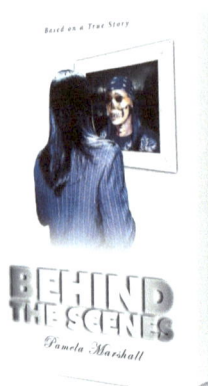

Behind The Scenes
By Pamela Marshall

Item #: BTS721
Price: $15.99

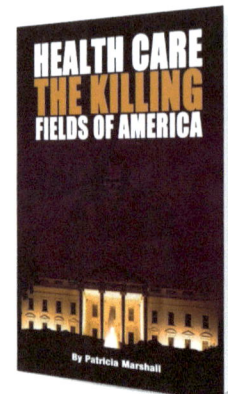

Health Care
By Patricia Marshall

Item #: HCTABF2
Price: $17.99

www.mocypublishing.com
order online and receive FREE shipping. Limit time offer.

YOU'LL FEEL ENERGIZED AND REJUVENATED IN JUST 20 MINUTES!

Physicians Supervised Programs for
Chronic Illnesses, Mega-Dose of Vitamin C and B Complex
Anti-Viral, Anti-Aging, Sports (Athletic Performance)
Detox (Drug and Alcohol), Joint Recovery, Energy/Vitality
Beauty Enhancement, & Bio-identical Hormone Replacement

NURTRITIONAL THERAPEUTIC IV INFUSIONS

CALL US FOR AN APPOINTMENT!
(586) 393-5439

MACOMB MEDICAL AND WELLNESS CENTER

27170 DEQUINDRE RD | WARREN MI 48092

WWW.MACOMBMEDICALWELLNESS.COM

REAL MUSIC. REAL ENTERTAINMENT.®

SDM LIVE

ISSUE 12

Also
PHILLY FAL
7MILE
RADIO
NO'EL
SNYDER
SARAH
APPLEB
LASURIA
"KANDI"
ALLMAN

NEW

KING DILLON
EXCLUSIVE P DOT

CHARLIE B. KEYZ
PUTTING IN MAJOR
LEGWORK IN THE
INDUSTRY

WWW.SDMLIVE.COM

TOYSOULJA
LAGOON
THE NEWEST
MEMBER OF
TEAM MONEY
HUNGRY

ORDER YOUR ISSUE FOR $9.99
Send money order plus $3.95 S&H to: Mocy Publishing, LLC
P.O. 35195 * Detroit, MI 48235

From Behide The Wall

WINNING TWO AWARDS WHILE INCARCERATED IS SOMETHING PEOPLE DREAM ABOUT, BUT NOT JP ONE AS HE COUNTDOWN THE DAYS TO FREEDOM

by JP ONE

What's good, SDM...It's JP ONE aka Jackpot Tha Chosen One aka Tha New Nigga You Love to Hate. I am currently inca-recerated in Milan (Federal Facility). I don't talk much about my time, but if you really wanted to know it's not hard to find out. The thing about the Feds is there is good time, programs and half-way house programs that will put me out a lot sooner than the computer says, so technically you won't know when I'm coming home until I'm almost there. The case is none of everybody's business, but if you are a real fan, you heard the "R.I.C.O." song and watched the documentary on my website www.jponelife.com and You-Tube. Basically, I am doing time for Conspiracy to Distribute Narcotics, though.

Although I have only been incarcerated a short period of time, I have been fighting this case for about two years. My closest family and friends were only aware of what I wanted them to be aware of, because the Feds play a totally different game. I have been reading a lot of business books and I'm getting ready to further my education by getting a business degree while I'm here. If you know me, you know I'm not one for wasting time. I want to thank everyone who has written me or emailed me and shown me love. If you are playing my music or sharing it on social media, I appreciate you. If you are acting like you are showing love to try to exploit my situation you will be held accountable. My fam is still my fam. I want to thank my lady, Lee Lee, and my niece, Layna Sky, for making sure my personal and business dealings are handled properly and my kids are taken care of. They are of the most importance to me. We are planning to continue to build the Gifted & Talented, LLC. brand by adding new team members and a few dope artists to the roster as soon as I return home.

We are continuing to build our network and ties within the music community in and outside of he city of Detroit. If you are trying to get in contact with me, you can message me via my personal and business FB pages and the information will be forwarded to me and a response will be delivered ASAP. You can also contact me directly via mail at:

Alvin C. Hill IV #51480039
4004 E. Arkona Rd.
Milan, MI 48160
#WESTILLWINNING

Send us your Mail Call:
P.O. Box 35195, Detroit Michigan. 48235

THE ALL NEW STYLE OF MAGAZINE-BOOKS

SDM LIVE ®

For advertisement
please call (833) SDM-LIVE
or visit www.sdmlive.com

www.ingramcontent.com/pod-product-compliance
Lightning Source LLC
Chambersburg PA
CBHW040018050426
42452CB00002B/37